The Home We Never Leave

The Home We Never Leave

poems by

Don Gutteridge

First Edition

Wet Ink Books
www.WetInkBooks.com
WetInkBooks@gmail.com

The Home We Never Leave
by Don Gutteridge

Cover Design – Richard M. Grove
Cover Photograph – Richard M. Grove
Layout and Design – Richard M. Grove

Typeset in Garamond
Printed and bound in Canada
Distributed in USA by Ingram,
  – to set up an account – 1-800-937-0152

Library and Archives Canada Cataloguing in Publication

Title: The home we never leave / poems by Don Gutteridge.
Names: Gutteridge, Don, 1937- author.
Identifiers: Canadiana 2022020909X | ISBN 9781989786635 (softcover)
Classification: LCC PS8513.U85 H56 2022 | DDC C811/.54—dc23

Contents

Kids At Play

The Home We Never Leave

It was a summer Saturday
when last I walked out upon
my town, silhouetted by the sun,
down Alexandra Ave,
under the Bridge with its gaunt
grey girders and cantilevered
leap above the blue
turbulence below, then across
the Marsh and its tufted, wind-
whetted rushes to the River
and its seething speed, around
the slow-dozing point to
Canatara's sylvan sands,
cradling the Lake and the
antediluvian dunes,
then drifting past the Slip,
where sailboats cantered
on their keels, and on to the
hedged edge of First Bush
and into its dappled depths,
where, here and there,
whenever a nugget of sunlight
leaked through the cullendered
canopy, a butterfly blinked
and a robin worried a worm,
and I was now arrived:
a circumnavigator
like Magellan or Drake, gallivanting
the globe – only to find
the home we never leave.

Kids At Play

Chanson Innocente

When the glow is gone from the
gloaming, we pour onto the
starlit streets like bats
riding a moonbeam,
boys and girls feathered
together: at home in their un-
corrupted bones, at ease
with their celibate dream, vexed
not by thought of sex
and the gnaw of its needs, hearkening
only to the half-mad
music of our hearts, glad
to be groomed, artless, by the dark.

Gumption

The sisters Laur are skipping
again on the walk next-door:
at first in listless, lazing
loops until someone
not their gender hollers,
"Hot pepper!" and their ropes
are then a quick-stepping,
blue blur against the
summer sky, hissing
the cement delicious, and when
they come to a hiccoughing halt,
they grin they give us lies
somewhere between girl-
gumption and wistful bliss.

Cartwheel

For Shirley McCord, friend of my youth

We start off the afternoon's antics
with somersaults on the
little hill that leans
greenly on Grandfather's lawn:
head-over-heels like tipsy
tumblers, again and again
until the world whirls
a-whee somewhere inside
where the eyes spy (and we can't
tell the clutter of cloud
from the swallow of sky) and when
the spinning's unspun,
Shirley struts downstage
with a tart toss of her tartan
and performs a perfect cartwheel,
thigh over unthumbed
thigh to the burst of the boys'
naughty applause.

Mumblety-Peg

I never had the nerve
(or the aim) to practice
mumblety-peg with chums
who were nimble with the knack
of knives (like Barnum-and-Bailey
pros), letting the unJacketed
blade whet a vivid
inch from the biggest toe,
but egged on by more pride
than sense, I put my fears
aside and, shameless, buried
the fine-boned blade
in the nearest foot, and thus
was my first game won.

My Dibs!

It wasn't Shakespeare or Ibsen,
but when a boyhood pal
or gal debouched from Granny's
larder with a bigger-than-bite-
sized cookie, our cry
of "My dibs!" laid
ineluctable claim
to some portion of that
munchable morsel, and needed
no further exegesis
or self-serving soliloquy.

Double-Doing

The girls are doing double-
Dutch on the walk next
door: Bonnie and Sharon
twirling the ropes in looped
ellipses, like a limp-wristed
showboat loosing his lariat,
while the one in the middle
does a two-footed
trot to the fiddle in her head,
eyes shut tight
against the hypnotic thrum
of hemp on cement, and there is
something ferociously female,
exotic or stalking in the entranced
dance of ropes and repetition,
as if something in the doing
has come undone.

Abracadabra

Point Edward 1947

On cold winter mornings
when the chill burns in the bone,
I join my chums (and others
less friendly) on the steps
of our school, where warmth beckons
behind the "BOYS" door
and, hands on the next fellow's
hip, we form a formidable
train and, rocking back
and forth, we hurl our collective
might against the impregnant
portal and, like Ali Baba
crying "Open sesame!"
we shout our own abra-
cadabra: "Warm beef!"
timed to the huff n' puff
rhythm of our ramming, and warmed
now all over, I feel
as chuffed as a pharaoh at ease
in his fiefdom.

Psalm

Our Grade Three class-
room was consigned to the
second floor, befitting
our lowly status, but we
could hear all the way
down the hall and all
the way down the wide
staircase to the principal's office,
(no bigger than a coffin)
where, on critical occasions,
some cringing, hapless
creature stood with upturned
palms (like a mendicant begging
for alms), and every slap
of the strap on that tender terrain,
every biblical blow
juddered our juvenile jaw-
bones and left us praying
for world peace and muttering
the twenty-third psalm.

On The Lam

I used to think that the
Post Office is a place
were folks old enough
to vote go each morning
at ten when the wicket winks
open to fetch their mail,
but I was mistaken, because
before I can say "Thank you,
ma'am," the game is afoot,
and Shirley's lips are inter-
spersing with mine, and blushing
like a bowdlerized bride, I take it
on the lam.

Red Rovering

When Bossy Betty calls me
over with her red-rovering
halloo and venom in her voice,
I am nothing if not nimble,
and make my dash for the
firing line where the biggest
brutes are bunched and brooding,
and throwing caution to the four
winds, I fling my boneless
body into the flotsam of the fray –
and am promptly tossed aside
like a whim or somebody' else's
afterthought.

Bottom

To the solitary hill in town,
feathered by the first flakes
of the season's snow, we take
our Santa Claus sleds
and birthday toboggans,
and one by one we launch them
like runaway, rudderless skis,
guiding them only with the
whim and wile of our bellies
and the need for the raptures of speed,
and soon, to the tune of our own
applause and like a yarn
without a plot, we go gliding
a-glee and agog, oohing and
aahing all the way down
to the bottomless bottom.

Eclipse

It was the girls who chose
to play Spin the Bottle,
and me, naive to the nines,
happily joined in,
and Shirley gave the conjugal
jug its first whirl,
and added a grin when it stopped
a vivid inch from my toe,
and the spectators giggled at our
flustered, hasty hug,
but the kiss that unpuckered
my lips was anything but chaste,
and something precious
had just been eclipsed in favour
of a new and sublime
ruckus of lip and lust.

Girl-Next-Door

Shirley, the girl-next-
door, twirls her baton
like a manic drummer on a
May-Day parade
and, tucked taut into her
tunic, struts her stuff
in tufted, white-laced
boots, and when she pirouettes
like a budding ballerina,
and there is only thigh
where skirt ought to be,
something tugs that shouldn't,
but when she sends my way
the smile of friendly affection
she's smiled before, she's once
again my girl-next-door.

Aerborne

When Leckie's fallow, after
January's thaw, freezes
over in a single, glistening
glaze, we lace our skates
in the crisp cold and, upright
under the condoning stars,
we begin our evening glide,
our steel-honed blades
stroking the ice with poised
precision and, marshalling
our breath's momentum
and soliciting speed, we sail
into the breeze our brows
allow, like whales endowed
with wings, until at last
we ride off the Earth's
edge and float free
of ourselves (airborne
in our bones.)

Grr

For Shirley McCord

How well I recall the days
when Summer thrummed in the blood
and Shirley next door
put the grr in girl
for me alone, and O
how I yearned for us to be
so much more than chums
(but didn't yet know
what the something else
was), even though
her smile set my bones
abuzz and dallied there,
for I was afraid, in beckoning
to her beguile, I might gain
some derring-do
but lose a pal.

Wounded

For my father in loving memory

I longed so much to be
the athlete my father was,
and though the War left us
separate, he came alive
for me in the news-clippings
he kept of his hockey heroics
in a thumbed scrapbook
I perused, wild with pride,
and when the Muse and I
finally met, I wanted
to paste his exploits in the
permanence of a poem, but wars
end and warriors come home,
wounded, and all too
human.

Mottled Mutt

At half-past five,
whatever the whims of the season.,
when Gramps had polished off
his supper, Bud, Missus
Bray's mottled mutt,
as if he were dinged by some
inner dinner-gong,
would cross the road anon,
negotiate the privet
and arrive just as Gran
was bending down, plate
in hand (dripping gravy
and miscellaneous leavings)
and lick it until the shine
unshone, and then
strut back home
like a dog from Dickens.

Rigs

It was a labour of love
when Grandfather fashioned
whirligigs, turned
on his workshop lathe
and sold to neighbours far
and near for a couple of dollars,
and on any Summer's evening
bathed in the lava of light,
all over town
you could hear the whispered whirring
of Grandpa's rigs, watering
leisurely lawns.

Road Trip

Each Summer morning,
whatever the shine of the sun,
my Gran headed for Burgess
Market a short block away,
to fetch her daily bread –
up the right aisle of Monk
in a sort of rolling stroll,
leaving room for a neighbourly
nod to Missus Shaw
next door, and pause
to chat of this and that
or drop a snip of gossip,
and on to pass the time
of day with Missus Hart,
widowed on her walk and,
coming back, down
the other aisle to say
a hearty hello to the second
Missus Shaw, whose news
and views deserved a good
airing, and on to Missus
Bray who, after all
was said and done, thought
'there aughta be' a law,'
and bearing left, her grocery-
load aloft, crossed
the road for home and a family
well fed.

Gentler

For Anne in loving memory

Long before I had a
daughter to dote on
and unsistered in my solitary
state, a brace of girls
drew for me the dimensions
of the gentler gender: Nancy
whom I worshipped from afar,
like Lancelot panting for Guin
and the Grail, or a lonely Galileo
sighting a star in the blur
of the firmament; and Shirley,
the girl-next-door
who batted her lashes as if
they mattered, put the verve
in flirt and the kissing in cousin,
and O how I wished I could find
the perfect feminine blend,
a middle ground where lust-for
and adore might mutually marry –
and a dozen years later,
I did.

Wild Surprise

My poems are merely lies
I rearrange to resemble
truth, and truth is what
we must surmise when nothing
else will do or when
we find ourselves estranged
from words and their ruthful wooing,
and I will tell it slant,
like Emily with her spinstered intuition,
and welcome its wild surprise.

Cindered

And there I was, a green
Grade Three, at sea
on the cindered schoolyard,
and wherever I gazed with exiled
eyes some vacant vista
gazed back at me,
and a big-hipped boy
was wielding a bat with muscled
menace and stalking a ball
whizzing his way, and further
afield, unhindered by hope
or symmetry, a scatter of like
combatants crouched in avid
expectation, and when the bat
cracked like a bone snapping
and the ball eloped to the prison
fence, I knew what it meant
to be lost and alone.

Delinquent

Christmas 1944

The Christmas in the aftermath
of my fever, my grandfather
carried me, like a delinquent doll,
into the front-room and set me
down on the green chesterfield
next to the decorated tree,
tingling with tinsel and ghostly
aglow, under which
was tucked a blood-red
firetruck my brother soon
rolled over the rug until
its lights blinked on
and something like an engine
purred, and I knew even then
that moments like these would find
a place in the poems that lay
inside like embardic bulbs,
a-seethe with meaning – waiting
their turn to breathe.

Aquiver

For Shirley McCord

Shirley was the first girl
on the block to cultivate curves,
bountiful bevels above
and below, all swerve
and sway, and we watched them
cling to the taut cloth
that swaddled them, and felt
something aquiver in the crotch
and an urge to defrock.

Alabaster

The blizzard blowing in
from the bellows of the Lake
with its hundred million filigreed
flakes, combs the contours
of the home landscape
with its white-wild whirl,
and leaves me dizzying
with doubt and as blind as
Macedonian Homer or Miltonic
Milton and inching ever
inward to the rarefied room
where dozing poems come
unfroze, breed delight, and burst
into alabaster bloom.

Melodious

The girls next door
are chanting "London Bridge"
and fitting actions to their words,
and the velvet of their voices drifts
my way as subtle as a mist
combing the gloaming, and when
they reach "my fair lady-o!"
their singing soars like a
coloratura's hitting
high-C, and I wonder
why it is that girls seem
to grow poetry in their bones
and have such a softness for song,
bringing with them the lullaby-lilt
that sang them once to sleep
and made them melodious.

Defiance

For Art Fidler

As an eight-year-old,
I never learned the secret
word for May-I? Ever
eager to please, I obeyed
the big bossy girl
directing traffic from above,
and, the consenting question
unremembered, happily
strode the designated steps,
like a new recruit sucking up to
the sergeant, and stunned to be
rebuked, I was in full,
chagrinned retreat, and O
how I longed just once
before I made it to nine,
to keep on walking, step
by giant step, defiant
to the end.

Caroms

At recess, in the sun-aglow
seasons, we erupt from the
wombed room of our school
like Monarchs fleeing a covey
of cocoons, and always the game
is Prisoner's Base, when we
gather in gendered regiments
on defended turf, waiting
for the first zigzagging rebel
to breech the Siegfried Line
and loose his troops among
the garrisoned girls (all flurry
and curls a-flung), and a knee
or two gets naughtily
nudged with a pardon-me
or a mischievous grin,
or a thigh surprises in the breeze,
or something more supple
above it gets covertly caromed,
and a need, too big
to undo, hungers in our blood.

Bubble

While the girls are doing
double-Dutch nearby,
their twinned ropes spinning
in looping lassoes like a
Dervish high on his hopes,
the boys are busy shooting
at aggies and allies and, better
still, cat's-eyes,
like marble-mavens, hunched
and hovering above a thumbed
boulder or brindled taw,
and sighting the prize (like Columbus
trawling for a star), and O the joy
when the glass assassin collides it
with a crisp click, and no-one
notes that the girls and the boys
are playing side by side,
each untroubled in their own
bachelor bubbles, waiting
for something *other*
to woo them.

Flotsam

The sisters Lauer are playing
bouncy-ball up against
the wall next door,
chanting "one, two, three
alairy" as they toss it
with limp-wristed ease
and just enough ounce
to bring it back home
to a faithful fist, and then
it's "leg over" with all
the poise of a primed ballerina,
and, with "clapsys" and "kneesys"
on to "eight, nine, ten"
and back again, like a
diva's recitative – and I am
enthralled by such ritual
rhythms and their hypnotic
erotics, by the chime and rhymes
of a chanting, fuelled by nothing
more than the fairy-flotsam
adream in the female mind.

Pebble

Sarnia Township: 1948

The girls next door
are drawing a hop-scotch
map their sisters drew
before them - on an unflawed
walk with a nubbed stub
of yellowing chalk – and the care
of a Mercator or any other
cartographer framing God's
geography, and soon
they will nimble, skirts a-swirl,
from square to square in long-
legged leaps – in pursuit
of a pebble and perfection, and when
they get there, the grin
they give the boys within
the beryl'd range of their gaze,
says: "Be amazed.
This is a girl's game
you practise at your peril."

Bobbing

Point Edward 1944

That fateful Halloween
Eve would have found me
bobbing for apples at Cubs'
club, pleased to be
a Sixer, chanting Akela
to our fearless leader like a
shaman weaving a spell
for the tribe, and I took
no note of the twinging
below until, heading
home, I felt my ankles
swell and prism with pain,
and I hobbled into our yard
like a cripple uncured by Christ
or a blind man uncertain
which dark to navigate,
and when I stepped inside
the welcoming warmth, the first
fronds of fever began
to burn rheumatic on my brow,
and soon I was consumed by an ache
I did not purge until it
unabided in the furied forge
of my poems.

Hankering

For Anne in loving memory

You love to drift asleep
on my shoulder, anchored in my arms,
and my breath floats in the halo
of your hair, and I love the way
your body bends to the semblance
of mine and surrenders its softness,
and it's as if we were twinned
double in some common,
untroubled womb, thigh
to thigh, our infant eyes
alive with the other's look,
and here we are in the rumpus
room, humbly hankering.

Feral

Sarnia Twp 1949

My gay brother, Bob,
has a way with the ladies,
idling on this soft
summer afternoon on the walk,
hobnobbing and talking
to the sisters Laur, as if
he were no threat and they had
no need to pretend
or rearrange their smiles,
and I am eaten with envy
at his bold beguiling of girls,
and wonder if their sexual
reticence has something to do
with me and manhood
or is simply the feral fear
of the *other.*

Blue

After reading Wallace Stevens

When the dark comes down
on a summer's town like a
leper's shrivelled shroud,
unmarred by the moon,
untarnished by stars,
the boys go rogue
and the girls live to regret,
and something septic
broods and brays (too
far to be gone),
and in an anguished alley
the Bogeyman strokes
his blue guitar.

Geranium

As long as I can remember,
my grandmother kept the blood-
bright geranium she nurtured
from seed in the living-room
window, where it could salvage
southern sunshine
in every breathing season,
and even though I couldn't say
she had a green thumb,
that perfect potted plant
with its livid leaves and upthrust
petals in the lick of light,
was just enough for me
to surmise how much love
is needed to keep us going.

The Daughters of Eve

It was Eve, our first female,
who took one look
at the daunting desmesne of Eden
(where flowers refused to grow
and trees latched onto
their leaves and bees were pleased
with the honey already combed
in the hive and birds were happy
to be bachelored) and made
a dash for the apple and all
it promised, and ever since,
her daughters have carried our water
and taken the biggest bites.

A Memorable Flight

Or how I lost my license
For my father, William Ernest
Charles Gutteridge, in loving memory

My Dad with his brand-new
pilot's license in his pocket
(a dream of his ever since
he pulled propellors for other
aviators and watched then soar
into glory) and a weakness for whisky
sits in an all-night
diner, high on the evening's
intake and boasting to the next
table of a Cessna 180
purring for him on the local
aerodrome, and would the young
buck there like to try
his luck, and off they go
effortlessly airborne, and Dad,
nodding off (and now
on cruise control) and comatose
on the stick, wakes up
just in time to smooth
into the boondocks of Hamilton,
grins and says to his hitch—
hiking friend (shocked
blue to the bone), "And that,
lad, is how it's done."

Big-Bellied

Towards the middle of March,
when the big-bellied breezes
blow in from the lung
of the Lake, we race to the
River Flats, homemade
kites in hand: Diamonds
and Deltas and Tiger Moths
with teeth, and Butch's buckles
in the fickle wind and Jerry's
wobbles like a ruptured duck
and gives up, and mine
catches a lucky gust
and soars high above
the Bridge where eagles dally
and dream of endless eddies
in the air, and I feel every
dip and dubious dive
in my two-fisted grip, as if
my soul were soaring in the
somewhere-beyond, and longed
to linger there.

Ogle

When I was young enough
to ogle girls for their coifs
and curls, I never guessed
the day would come when I would
calibrate the bevelling
of a breast, or wonder what lay
furled in that Vestal vee,
or wish the look they gave
the guys were ripe and roguish.

Bolder

My brother Bob, always
bolder than me, sweet-
talks Marilyn into lifting
her skirts and dropping her drawers,
and when she begs him do
likewise, he pulls out
his "dink" and watches it throb,
and when the gulled girl
bares it all, I try,
between blushes and flushes,
not to show my surprise
at the shy, unfeathered fold
dividing her thighs: a pinkling
bud you'd rather hug
than plug.

An Argument
Sarnia Twp: 1948

My best friend, Tommy,
averred the world was flat
and that, if he dug down
far enough, he would hit
water or China or a dinosaur's
den, and when I informed him
dinas were derelict and Earth
was a ball I could walk around
quicker than he could dig,
hie big brother, Glenn,
said Tommy's talk was rot
and mine just jargon –
thereby settling the argument.

Himalayan

Our Himalayan puss
was all fur and fine
fettle, affronted no doubt
at being called "Cookie,"
(when her antecedents had curled
up on the laps of Hapsburgs
and potentates and Bengali
gurus) and purred only
when stroked or dinner was served,
and she took a decided dislike
to me and others of the gentleman
gender, pouncing at night
on my pillow or any part
of the bed I tried to over-
occupy or lay my head,
and on sunny days she could be
seen sprawled on the hot
walk, paws upthrust,
fluffed belly begging
to be rubbed, until; some
friend of toms and tabbies
happened by and, smiling
all the while, reached down
to give kitty a caress,
and found himself in a four-
clawed grip – still,
I must confess I admired
her feline guile and gall,
her bemused refusal to be
anybody's pet.

A Dog's Life

My dog Moochie was a
web-pawed water-
spaniel affronted by water,
whether in the drainage ditches
or sudden puddles when the rain
relented, and although he had a
nose for news of anything
edible, the only prey
he tracked, like a hound on a crippled
hare, was me and the gang
on the road to school a mile
or more away, and the girls
would shout, "Moochie, go home!"
which command he took
as canine encouragement
to wag his tail and carry on
to Leckie's farm, where their mongrel
mastiff chomped on his chain,
and thence to S.S. 12,
where my pooch patiently
waited beside the Boys'
entrance, like an orphaned elf,
until the morning ebbed
and the noon-sun hovered,
bringing musty crusts
and a flotsam of tossed bologna-
bits, and he does his best
to "sit" and, when pressed,
"roll over," as if to say,
"This is a dog's life
and what we do to be loved.."

Young Still

Guelph, Ontario: February 1961
For Anne in loving memory

It was an ordinary Winter's
evening: the stars were a crystal
target, cushioned by the cold,
and the moon, hung above
like a gilded doubloon, lets
its light idle in your eyes,
and like a pilgrim at prayer, I fold
your hand in mine, and we are
happy to be here on this
numinous night, brimming
inside us, our love
still young.

Fishing Paradise

Cameron Lake: Summer 1996
For Tom in loving memory

I remember well our afternoons
cruising Cameron for big-
mouthed bass in their underwater
undulations, all sinew
and ribbed fin and lethal
lurking, while around us
the Lake: consuming light,
licked limpid by the merest
breath of a breeze and, on every
side: bark-bleeding
birch, fletched fir
and drooping spruce see
themselves adream in the
blue-below, and something
with bulk and bravado tugs
on your line, and you rise up
with the rod in your grip like a young
god fishing Paradise,
unruffled by His Nibs' stare,
and I knew even then
that Death has its own devises
and love is never enough.

Aerie

Fourth Line, Sarnia Twp, 1948

From my lofted window, like an
eagle from its aerie, I watch
the distant ploughman lope
behind his pair of matched
Percherons, and steady the throbbing
blade with a manly, two-
handled grip, like a water-
witching wizard pulled
along by underground urges,
and behind him, the cleft loam
of the fallowed field uncurls
like spun ribbon, and cowbirds
flurry it for worms and grubs
and a kildeer, eloped from home,
keens on wind-wobbled
wings – and something inside me
soothes, and sings.

Artless

For Nancy Mara, friend of my youth:
Point Edward, 194/

On my regular route to Canatara,
I have to pass the Slip,
where sailboats bend
in the breeze, and un-swimmers
(like me) have but a slim
chance of surviving its lethal
deep, and on an improvised
board, Nancy Mara
prepares to dive, and flings
herself upward and out,
like an antelope halfway
thru its leap, and hangs
for a frozen moment like an aerialist
in love with his trapeze or Blondin
atilt on the rim of his rope,
and she cleaves the sudden surface
with the smooth swoon of her
bourgeoning girl-body,
leaving no trace
of her artless entry - and, bereft
of hope, I want to follow her
down, and drown.

Wide-Eyed

My buddy, Butch, who keeps
the bullies away, lets me
ride side-saddle on his brand-
new CCM,
and we cut thru Hendrie's alley,
outwitting Constable Pedan
on his beat, looking to put
the brakes on boyhood bliss,
and when the breeze we cleave
with our quick skedaddle touches
something flooding mischievous
inside us, I feel like Adam
must have felt, waking up,
wide-eyed, in Eden.

Cartwheel

For Shirley McCord, friend of my youth

We start off the afternoon's antics
with somersaults on the
little hill that leans
greenly on Grandfather's lawn:
head-over-heels like tipsy
tumblers, again and again
until the world whirls
a-whee somewhere inside
where the eyes spy (and we can't
tell the clutter of cloud
from the swallow of sky) and when
the spinning's unspun,
Shirley struts downstage
with a tart toss of her tartan
and performs a perfect cartwheel,
thigh over unthumbed
thigh to the burst of the boys'
naughty applause.

A Caroming Of Carols

Christmas 2021

Christmas Eve, and the snows
come down like a benediction
upon gable, eave and sill
and lay an alabaster limn
on the last of the Autumn grass,
and it is the season of Jesus
and the miracle of manger and virgin
birth and Peace on Earth
(for heretic or heathen or not)
and into the silence of the star-
strummed streets: the caroming
of carols and the belling of a dozen
believing steeples and voices
vivid with faith in a universe
worth loving, bending to the will
of something that breathes
beyond our bones and leaves us
unalone.

Fifth Season

For Tom in loving memory

Five seasons have passed
since you last drew breath:
the Summer that you died
all living things succumbed
with a sympathetic sigh
and said their green goodbyes,
and in the Autumn that ensued,
the seed-seething breeze
unhummed like a dimuending
dirge, and that Winter
no snows flurried or flung
and no winds arose
to sanctify the silence or cozy
the cold, and when Spring
finally arrived, its bulbous
bloat rubbed ribald
by the rain, my grief gathered
again and settled there
until the second Summer
come, where June's bloom
was wrought anew to simmer
in the sun, and you were not.

Repute

With a nod to John Keats

When I have fears that I may
cease to please my muse,
when dactyls no longer dance
and anapests pause for breath
and the motive for metaphor eludes
collusion, I simply think
of all the years when poems
flowed boneless into being:
imprudent, renegade, happily
heretic – but still, I yearn
for one last time
to dip my quill in delinquent
ink and fashion lines
lustrous enough to live
in passionate repute beyond
my allotted days and desultory
death.

Aglow

On a summer's afternoon,
when the grass was thinking
of giving up its green,
Shirley arrives on Grandfather's
lawn, high-stepping
in her tufted alabaster boots,
an underage majorette
with a sumptuous strut
that left my heart a-stutter
and something further below
aglow.

Unsaid

For Anne and for Tom, in loving memory

Benumbed by the thought of all
that I have lost, I summon up
scenes of childhood longagos
I can never fully retrieve,
but even a glimpse of those
innocent images brings them
flooding back: of a would-be
boy-bard, trawling
Grandfather's yard
for something akin to simile,
stirred by words that seethed
inside, bred in the bone
and sought solace in the tellings
no other tongue had yet
extolled, as if the poems
I would someday compose
with a wild beguiling, ought
to leave their best sense
unsaid.

That Night

You were hardly turned five
that momentous night
when snowflakes feather
windless in the air and brushed
our cheeks alive, and we found
a little toboggan run
in Gibbon's, squeezed between
young evergreens, ike the apse
of a lapsed chapel, and we rode
your heathen "Whees!" all the way
down to the bottomless bottom,
hugged numinous in the snow-
dazzled dark, and somewhere
high above, where love
has its being, a gibbous moon
comes unbibbed, and blooms.

Blithe Bevel

When snows come down
like feathered fleece on ell
and eave and sill, and layer
the last of the grass with an
alabaster buffing, we don
our winter togs and tug
Christmas toboggans,
siblings aboard, to the
only hill in town,
but it is high enough
to please a bombardier
or ten tipplers on a trapeze,
and we glide agog down the
wind-quickened track
on the blithe bevel of our bellies,
breeze-bitten and free
to dream of weather-winged
flight and eagles, like argonauts
arrowing the air.

My Big-Boned Boy

For Tom in loving memory

You were such a big-boned
bountiful boy with your
cinnamon locks and azure
eyes, and I remember the day
I saw you first on skates
with your gliding, sturdy strides
and the hockey-stick, like a fillip
of flotsam in your four-fingered
grip, and when your team
switched ends, you startled
the skeptics in the crowd (and me)
by bearing down on your own
goal like a locomotive
breathing steam and looking
for rails to ride, and brushing
aside the whoops and catcalls
and frantic defencemen and all
attempts to alter your craftful
cruising, and the move you made
on your stunned netminder
would have occasioned kudos
from Rocket Richard, and it is
memories like these that bless
and buoy whenever I think
of what the world lost
when you took yourself (and joy)
out of it.

Unaided

And so, as a last resort,
I try bob-skates with their sturdy
double-bladed purchase,
and scrape my way across
Grandfather's Christmas rink,
unaided in a wobbling,
graceless glide that is
finally aborted by the bank
on the other side – and I am
grateful my Dad is still
away at the wars.

Voluminous

I must have heard, still
welcome in the womb, some
word other than the thrum
of my mother's blood in verbal
bloom, because when my lungs
first occupied air,
the cry they flung into the
megaphone of my throat
was a solitary syllable that stunned
the room, a vowel voluminous
and uncluttered by consonance,
a slow, exploding burst
of breath, imbued with its own
surmise, the unassailable
"Oh!" I would use to utter
my world aloud.

Something Dies

With every line I write,
something in me dies
before it blooms, as the sun
must set before its shine
re-arrives or the moon
glower before it gleams
anew, as if whatever
we love consumes the lustre
that lit it, as if the words
I purge from the purgatory of the page
were born from our unembuable
blood and lost belonging, as if
there were no room in the bardic
womb for anything other
than doing and dying.

Huggable

In the days before Internet
porn or gaudy mags
with silicone centrefolds,
in our gnawing need to know
what goodies prowled beneath a
                              buttoned blouse, we had
to be happy with our imaginings
(do they droop, or pout or point?)
or the prurient pages of catalogue
petticoats, and we dreamed
of snuggling up to whatever
delights might be on offer –
and utterly huggable.

Harbour

For Tom in loving memory

My grief is like a
moon-tugged tide
that ebbs and flows but never
leaves the sea: an ache
that bivouacs in the bone
and throbs like a robin's thrum,
frozen in the throat, or a bloated
bruise unbuttoning in the blood
like the venom of a viper, but I
welcome such bereavement
pain in its greed to glutton
on grief, because it lets you
live again where love itself
resides: in the much-hugged
harbour of the heart, and if
I were to believe in Paradise
and all that that implies,
and you were there before me,
waiting, it would be a relief
to die.

Root

When Paradise was come
undone through Eve's
over-ample appetite,
she was newly gloomy,
but Adam, savouring the scenery,
was glad-ish, and soothed her soul
by rooting in her radish.

Bewildered

I'd love to compose a poem
that would burst aloud like a
blood-blister exploding
in the bone, or float like a rose
in leavening light, seasoned
with similes and ept with metaphor
and voluminous enough to envelope
a village and its gendered denizens,
then last so long as the morning
sun stuns the world awake
or the moon endeavors to gild
the gloaming with its glistened glow,
and when I'm done, I'll let
my words return to the
Great Lexicon in the sky,
be-still my quivering quill,
and leave this life as bewildered
as it was when first begun.

Baubles

When God said, "Let there be
light!" He bade it varnish
the verdure of Eden, and incite
everything green to ignite,
and each bachelor bulb
rupture bruised into bloom,
and all was serene and settled
until Eve noticed her nakedness
and checked the heft of Adam's
sampler, and the newly nuptialed
couple gobbled on apples
that hung like bloated baubles
from the Knowing Tree, begging
to be bitten

Lucid: October 1996

For Tom in loving memory

Walking the woods above Cyprus
with Tom on an early autumnal
morning, where we are greeted
by a flicker's tick-tocking
thrum, and in the odd
pockets of sunshine
butterflies tilt on wind-
hinged wings, and at our feet,
wild orchids in the undergrowth
harvest the dark, and a rattler
unravels in the welter of warmth,
and blue jays jabber
like jumped-up gossips,
and the last of the summer bees
convene in the hive and disembark
the drones, and down by the marsh
marigolds gather in golden
galore, and bullfrogs
strum the hum in their throat
and cattails frazzle, and we are
here, unwearied in the wonder
of our walking, for we are embowelled
by Beauty and thumbed lucid
by love.

Double-Bricked

Grandfather's house was built
of sandstone, double-bricked –
about the time the last
century wakened to the world,
with wide, roofed verandahs
fore and aft, and two
tall trees shepherded
shade where the summer sun
licked and stung, and the 'back
forty' meandered on
like a manicured meadow,
limned by lilac-hedges
in bridal bloom, and the image
of this perpetual place
shook my stanchions like the
ransacking stanzas
of an apprentice poem, but I was
young enough then
to let it bubble in the blood
and settle in the bone.

Mystical

For Anne in loving memory

There is something mystical about
a midnight stroll along
Canatara's ante-
diluvian sands, barefoot
in rollers that sigh and subside,
like mist fretting in the wind,
with a majestic moon above us
like a golden oval, orphaned
young in the star-strummed
dark, and I take your hand
in mine like a pilgrim polishing
a shrine, and somewhere
in the far fastness of the firmament,
the green-eyed gods seethe,
and we know that dream-demesnes
like this cannot last, though we
defy the envying odds
just by being here,
together or alone, letting
the pristine gist of the evening
breathe in our bones.

High Hover

It's a summer Saturday
and Coop and I take
turns flicking the reins
over the heaving flanks
of the sibling Clydes, hoofing
ahead between stooked rows,
sheaves a-droop in limpid
mist, and under the rumble
of the wagon's wheels and the clatter
of the whiffletrees, a kildeer
keens, a crow chides
from its high hover, and cow-
birds squabble over spilt
milk, and we wend our way
through the subdued swoon
of the afternoon, praying
that a day like this should never
end.

Unaltered

Seventy years on
and I can still recall
the kids who kindled delight
in my boyhood days:
Shirley, the girl-next-door,
who set my heart alight;
Butch, the big brother
I never had, who kept
the bullies at bay; Nancy,
who drifted through my dreams
like a lodestone of loveliness
and stirred in me visions
of Lancelot and graceful Gwen;
Wiz Withers, who dazzled
our gang with gizmos and gadgets
galore; and Jerry Mara,
who swam like Tarzan's twin
and simply let me be me;
and I hope to meet them all
in Heaven – unaltered.

Collision

For Anne in loving memory

In one small, windowed
room, with sunshine on the sill
by day and moonglow
blooming by night, we lay
as lovers have lain ever
since Adam took Eve
in bevelled embrace and bartered
Eden for other delights,
and in the misted aftermath
of our carnal collision, I brush
your brow with my pilgrim lips,
kiss your lids alight,
bend your breath to the brink
of mine, and revel in the bliss
our bodies engender.

Sizzle

If Adam was puffed from dust,
and Eve ripped from a
random rib, did
their Maker mold them as
His and Hers, each
with their own equipment –
with a prudent eye on procreation
(should Eden ever fizzle)
or was it merely for the
sexual sizzle?

Miraculous

For Tom in loving memory

With an anxious eye, I watch
you make your maiden manoevres
on ice: taking a first
tip-toe, glacial
glide, just this side
of gravity's grip, followed
by a wobble as wee as a wink,
and then you are striding, stroke
by stroke, skating as if
you were born to the sport, and I can
feel you seeking the soothing
thrum of equilibrium,
when brain and body un-
becumber, and what I didn't know
then was that such miraculous
moments would keep me enthralled
for thirty-five years,
until Death robbed us both:
you of breath and me
of miracles.

Praise Enough

Missus Bray's garden
was groomed by the god she prayed to
every night and in the
listless mists of morning,
when Heaven's dew dappled
daffodil or daisy, or the bee-
teased breeze plucked
at petal or pod, and the laudatory
nod of a passerby or two
was praise enough for a life
filled with the bliss of perpetual
bloom.

Cat's Meow

For Tom in loving memory

From the moment I spied you
curled in your crib and you
sized me up with your baby
blues, I liked the cut
of your jib, and you soon
became for me His Nibs,
the cat's meow, the bees
knees and the farmer dancing
in his dell – and somewhere
in our reciprocated gaze,
two souls fused,
and I hitched my wagon to yours,
caring not that such
unblinkered love comes
with a cost, when Death ruptures
the rapture like ribs ripped
from the body still breathing,
left alone with a grief
burrowed in the bone, while the gods
look on, blood on their bibs.

Ah, Love

For Anne in loving memory

Ah, love, let us linger
in the light made brighter
by the dark that cradles it,
for we were young enough
to know better and let
our bodies blend, as sunshine
knows the rose or a breeze
luffs on a leaf, and for you
I would lasso the moon
or unstartle the stars,
and bring them down to illume
the bloom, harvesting in my heart,
and ladle the Earth with the joy
it engenders.

Nightmare

The night after we watched
Grace's roan stallion
mount the mare and plant
his almighty muscle into
her nuptial notch, I dreamed:
not of the smile that made
my heart stutter, but of gelded
girls in bloated embrace
and intimate urges in iodized
eyes as glittered as gold
medallions.

Daffodillian

When the Reverend Bell waxed
bromidic about that first
Garden, where every flower
was stunned lovely by the
sacerdotal sun,
I merely let my gaze graze
Missus Bray's bouquet'd
bower, where blossom and bloom
were doted on with a
Pentecostal fervour
and coaxed to grow in a
daffodillian daze,
and when the last knell
has died away, the Missus
will be found plucking posies
in Paradise.

Rubicund

For Anne in loving memory

O, my love, you were a
rubicund rose, soothed
anew by the celibate sun,
a-bloom in the perfumed brew
of the breeze, and I would build you
a bower where every flower
is fuelled by fancy and every
petal does a dithyramb-dance,
and wherever you are, hither
or yon, whole or asunder,
hope flows and love
lives.

Wonder

When I was young enough
to know better, I wondered
if bees sneezed or butter-
flies blushed or my uncle
took snuff, but pretty soon
I grew too wise
for my years, and what I wondered,
then, is where the wonder
went.

Coif

When I was still in thrall
to Sunday school and its tall
tales of biblical saints
and sinners, I pictured Satan
as a sly serpent in a sequined
three-piece suit
with a pomaded part in his quiffed
coif, an eye for the ladies
and the rictus of a grin, who bellied
into the groomed groves
of Eden and sweettalked Eve
into apprehending the Apple,
while God in His Pentecostal pod
looked on, unamused.

Two for Marybelle

That Day

I fell in love the day
Marybelle Cooper leaned
across our picket fence
in her tartan vest, beneath
which, her newly-minted
breasts breathed like a pair
of doting doves in serene
repose, and when she smiled
my way, I was cock-a-
hoop and my tongue tied.

Bevels

Marybelle Cooper lays
her lithe loveliness along
Canatara's sun-thumbed
sands in her one-piece
suit, a-swell with hummocks
and hillocks and bevels
in prurient places my gaze
engages, and I don't yet know
what lust can be or do,
and I'm chuffed enough to holler
Hallelujah, sing till I
scintillate, mime The Lord's
Prayer, and tithe.

Voluptuous

Adam and Eve were fashioned
each with a sexual apparatus
and no clue how to arrange
the rigging, until Eve
munched on a MacIntosh,
and the newly nuptialed couple,
abashed to be unduly
nude, soon developed
an appetite for fig-fronds
and peaches in voluptuous bunches.

Bee-Dream

When Emily died, she heard
a fly buzz nearby,
like a muted trumpet, heralding
Heaven, and when I go,
unwilling, the way of all
flesh, I hope to hear
a bee's behemoth buzz,
loud enough to shake
my bones awake and remind
my severed soul of pollen-
dusted bloom in gardens,
where poppies thrive in petalled
puffs and daisies blow
in a beckoning breeze like stars
unstrung from the dark,
and roses explode, lustered
by light, and gilded gladioli
gleam like surrogate suns,
and I will take the buzz
and its delights with me
into the bee-dream
of Paradise.

Glories

Missus Bray's June
garden without a breath
of breeze is nonetheless
a-thrum with bee-buzz
among the pollinated petals
of peonies as pink as a
bride's blush and poppies
a-swoon in the lacquered light
and daisies still damp
from the dew and mums
in multicoloured dozens,
and on a far arbour,
baby-fisted roses
pose in bountiful bouquet
like the gist of the sweetening season —
and no-one since Adam
adumbrated Eden
has ever seen such
horticultural glories.

Blot

Citizen Cain was born
with a blemish, a blot
too black to be labbelled
'sable,' and it must have been
ordained, if you believe
in such babble, that Cain
slay Abel.

Epithalamium

For Anne, wherever you are

Our joy consists in this:
seeing ourselves buoyed
in the other's eyes, purged
of all passions we dare not
deny, and we are linked
as twins are woven in the womb,
as bride-and-groom are coupled
in nuptial nurture, and we
shall grow old together
in our comfortable pews,
(while the world turns on a word
and the moon looms), humbled
as we are by a love that feeds
on the bliss it breeds.

Sunset: Southampton, 1978

On the far Western rim
of my soft-summering world,
where the blue of the Lake
and the blue of the sky quietly
collide, the last blast
of sunlight seethes
before its long day's
dying, kept aloft
by the hues it flings up
into the cotton-bellied
nimbi, hovered above,
and sprays across the languid
luff of the Lake like an
oriental carpet, culled
from the Caucasus and pied
with petalled pinks, muted
mauves and yellows as mustard
as a picaroon's doubloons,
and I watch them boil like blood
on a gibbous moon, sink
beneath the breathless brim,
and blink out, like a ruptured
star.

Jig

When Adam and Eve realized
they were nude in each other's
eyes, who made the first
move to the fig tree
and its shame-shunning leafage,
and did Eve linger a look
at his romantic rigging
or did Adam glance too
long where no man's
glance belonged? And when
the figs were primly in place,
was it too late for
sedate relations? Was the jig
already up?

Lilt

For Tom in loving memory

My feelings for you run
like the dark is really light,
untouched by love,
and my bereavement pain
lets me know at least
that I'm alive, and just
the thought of you, somewhere
at ease, warms me
like a bee honeyed in the hive,
and lifts me free and afloat,
like a bird, feathered by flight,
and you drift through my dreams
like a simulacrum of my soul
and leave them lilting.

O What A Time!

For Anne in loving memory and
with a nod to Edmund Spenser

O! what a time that was
when we wooed and then wed
and brought ourselves to the
marriage-bed, and I read you
a ream of Spenserian rhyme,
in which the bride's breasts
were wrought as clotted cream
and nipples tipped with berry-
buds and lips as 'rudded'
as apples sweetened in the sun –
but we laced our love, instead,
with the honey-hive of affection,
pleased as bees with their buzz.

Bits

When Eve, upended from Eden,
awoke in the nether-below,
she lay upon the dappled
grass and wondered what
breasts were for, or whether
the furred furrow at her thigh
ought not to be throbbing,
and when Adam swaggered by,
all brawn and bravado,
with interesting bits here
and there, she didn't know
which bit was which
or how in the world to grapple them.

Don Gutteridge was born in Sarnia and raised in the nearby village of Point Edward. He taught High School English for seven years, later becoming a Professor in the Faculty of Education at Western University, where he is now Professor Emeritus. He is the author of more than seventy books: poetry, fiction and scholarly works in pedagogical theory and practice. He has published eighty books; twenty-two novels, including the twelve-volume Marc Edwards mystery series, and forty seven books of poetry, one of which, Coppermine, was short-listed for the 1973 Governor-General's Award. In 1970 he won the UWO President's Medal for the best periodical poem of that year, "Death at Quebec."

Don lives in London, Ontario.

519-873-1585
gutteridgedonald@gmail.com